The Practice of the Presence of God

A 40-Day Devotion
Based on Brother Lawrence's
The Practice of the Presence of God

Book by Brother Lawrence
Devotions by Alan Vermilye

The Practice of the Presence of God
A 40-Day Devotion Based on Brother Lawrence's
The Practice of the Presence of God

Copyright © 2021 Alan Vermilye
Brown Chair Books

ISBN-13: 978-1-948481-19-9

To learn more about this book and other Bible study resources by the
author visit **www.BrownChairBooks.com**.

Version 1

Contents

Free Bible Study Supplement

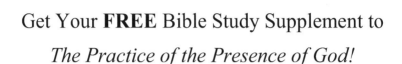

Get Your **FREE** Bible Study Supplement to
The Practice of the Presence of God!

Includes:

Small Group Discussion Guide

The Spiritual Maxims of Brother Lawrence

The Life of Brother Lawrence

www.BrownChairBooks.com/Practice

Introduction

WHO IS THIS BROTHER LAWRENCE? And, why should I care about what a monk, who lived over 300 years ago, said about creating a closer relationship with God? Afterall, I'm not a monk. I don't live in a monastery blocked off from the harsh realities of the real world. Things are different today. Times have changed. I cannot sit around all day reading my Bible and chanting some nonsense. I live in the here and now with responsibilities and people that count on me.

At least this is the way it sounded in my head as I made excuses for and questioned whether a book that has been read, studied, and adored by countless Christians over centuries had any validity for a Christ follower today.

So, I committed to read *The Practice of the Presence of God*—a collection of notes, letters, and interviews given by Lawrence to show how to develop a conversational relationship with God. Then I reread it. It's not a long book and is easily digestible so it was not a hard read. But each time I read it, I did so under the pre-conceived notions mentioned above. In other words, I came loaded for bear. It did not stand a chance! Sure, if I were a monk with nothing to do all day but a few chores in the confines of a peaceful monastery, I too could spend all day in the presence of God!

But after further reflection, maybe I was being too harsh. The only way I was really going to understand the value of this classic piece of literature was to set aside any judgement and analyze it honestly. That's exactly what I did. And in doing so, I felt a growing awareness of just how wrong I was. All my pre-conceived notions were an oversimplification of Brother Lawrence's life and how he developed a conversational relationship with God right in the middle of an ordinary life. Who was I to judge whether his life was any more ordinary than mine!

Yes, Brother Lawrence was a monk, but he was not born in a monastery. Prior to taking his vow, he was a poor peasant who became a soldier in a brutal war and probably saw more carnage and death than we could imagine. He was not immune to the sufferings of life and had many scars, both physical and spiritual, to prove it.

Regarding his faith, he was not overly righteous. Like the Apostle Paul, he considered himself the worst of sinners. Ironically, he never sought to publish a book with instructions for the Christian community, rather he was simply corresponding by letters and interviews with a friend about the depth of his love for God. In fact, he even requested that this information not be shared. He probably would have been mortified to know that his friends published his story and the workings of his spiritual practice after his death in 1691.

And finally, I don't believe Brother Lawrence was providing prescriptive instructions to the Christian believer. It's not a one size fits all. He was simply stating to his friend some tried and true practices that helped him create a deep, abiding connection with his Creator.

You will find most of his methods rooted in Scripture although he does not quote one verse. And although you might disagree with him on some finer points, overall, I think you will find his ways fairly accurate and timeless. In the very least, it worked for him.

If you really want to save time, I can summarize the book for you like this: To really know, understand, and love God, you must spend time with Him…a lot of time!

However, I think my summary cheapens the deep spiritual wisdom that Brother Lawrence offers to his dear friend. It's one thing to understand a spiritual concept, but a whole other thing to practice it. Like any sport, if you want to get better, you must practice with people who are better than you, and Brother Lawrence was an all-star!

The Practice of the Presence of God is a public domain work and not hard to find. A quick search on the Internet will pull up many downloadable copies with a ton of commentary to boot.

What you will not find are many devotionals based on the content of this classic. Therefore, I've laid out a 40-day devotional format with related Scripture passages that will hopefully provide a better understanding of Brother Lawrence's message and overall book. Why 40 days? Well, it's biblical, but more importantly, it fit very well when I laid out the book! Each devotion contains an excerpt from Brother Lawrence, a Scripture reference to read, and a short reflection on the passage. I've also included the entire book of *The Practice of the Presence of God* in the back. I would encourage you to read it each day alongside your devotions.

You might have noticed that this book is offered for free. Well, at least the e-book is on most platforms. For some time, I've wanted to provide a free book as a gift to everyone who has participated in any of my studies. For those who prefer print, I've kept the price as low as possible, but there are printing and retailer costs that must be covered. However, I still think you'll find it an excellent value!

You will also find a free Bible study supplement online at www.BrownChairBooks.com/practice. The supplement includes a discussion guide for individual and small group use, *Spiritual Maxims* (or life lessons) by Brother Lawrence, and a more detailed biography titled *The Life of Brother Lawrence* written by his friend Joseph de Beaufort.

I hope you will enjoy this devotional as much as I enjoyed writing it! If you are new to my studies, you can learn more about those resources in the back of this book.

Now for my normal disclaimer. I'm not an expert on the life of Brother Lawrence nor his work, I will leave that to well apt scholars. However, I hope this work will help you set aside any pre-conceived notions you might have about this timeless Christian classic as you meditate over Brother Lawrence's work, life, and related Scriptures in the midst of the challenges you face today.

Day 1: Becoming Wholly God's

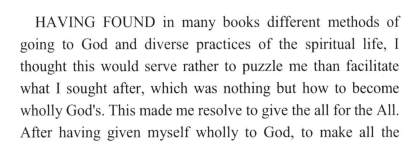

HAVING FOUND in many books different methods of going to God and diverse practices of the spiritual life, I thought this would serve rather to puzzle me than facilitate what I sought after, which was nothing but how to become wholly God's. This made me resolve to give the all for the All. After having given myself wholly to God, to make all the satisfaction I could for my sins, I renounced, for the love of Him, everything that was not He, and I began to live as if there was none but He and I in the world. – *Letter 1*

1 Corinthians 2:15-16

Imagine a world with just you and God. In this world, you have a present, personal, and indisputable sense that He is all yours and you are all His. Obviously, in the real world you are not alone, but consider for a moment what would change in your life if you were to adopt this mindset. A mindset where the love of everything not Him fades away, freeing you to offer yourself wholly to God. Adopting a "mind of Christ" attitude of continual submission to God enables us to live confidently, joyously, and sacrificially each day.

Day 2: Think About Such Things

SOMETIMES I CONSIDERED myself before Him as a poor criminal at the feet of his judge. At other times I beheld Him in my heart as my Father, as my God. I worshipped Him the oftenest I could, keeping my mind in His holy presence and recalling it as often as I found it wandered from Him. I made this my business, not only at the appointed times of prayer but all the time; every hour, every minute, even in the height of my work, I drove from my mind everything that interrupted my thoughts of God.

I found no small pain in this exercise. Yet I continued it, notwithstanding all the difficulties that occurred. Though I have done it very imperfectly, I have found great advantages by it. – *Letter 1*

Isaiah 26:3; Philippians 4:8

What consumes your mind controls your life. Today, try asking God to free you from anxious thoughts and to remind you of all that is commendable and good while keeping your heart fixed on Jesus—not just during prayer time, but all day long.

Day 3: Hindered or Free?

WHEN WE ARE FAITHFUL to keep ourselves in His holy presence, and set Him always before us, this hinders our offending Him, and doing anything that may displease Him. It also begets [creates] in us a holy freedom, and, if I may so speak, a familiarity with God, where, when we ask, He supplies the graces we need. Over time, by often repeating these acts, they become habitual, and the presence of God becomes quite natural to us. – *Letter 1*

Hebrews 12:1; Galatians 5:13

Think of one thing in your life that displeases God. Whatever that is, it's undermining your ability to keep yourself in His holy presence. Now, imagine the freedom you will experience if you yield to the promptings of the Holy Spirit and begin to obey Christ in that area of your life. The more time spent in His presence, the more familiar we become with Him, and the less likely we are to do things that displease Him.

Day 4: Renouncing All for Him

IN CONVERSATION SOME days ago a devout person told me the spiritual life was a life of grace, which begins with servile [submissive] fear, which is increased by hope of eternal life, and which is consummated by pure love; that each of these states had its different steps, by which one arrives at last at that blessed consummation.

I have not followed these methods at all. On the contrary, I instinctively felt they would discourage me. Instead, at my entrance into religious life, I took a resolution to give myself up to God as the best satisfaction I could make for my sins and, for the love of Him, to renounce all besides. – *Letter 2*

Luke 14:33; Philippians 3:8

Brother Lawrence was told that the spiritual life progressed through three stages beginning with fear, then to hope of eternal life, and finally to pure love. He was frustrated by these methods and was determined to focus only on giving himself completely to God. In other words, if he must choose between Christ and anything else, he would choose Christ. Which method are you following?

Day 5: Always Before Me

YET I MUST TELL YOU that for the first ten years I suffered a great deal. During this time, I fell often, and rose again presently. It seemed to me that all creatures, reason, and God Himself were against me and faith alone for me.

The apprehension that I was not devoted to God as I wished to be, my past sins always present to my mind, and the great unmerited favors which God did me, were the source of my sufferings and feelings of unworthiness. I was sometimes troubled with thoughts that to believe I had received such favors was an effect of my imagination, which pretended to be so soon where others arrived with great difficulty. At other times I believed that it was a willful delusion and that there really was no hope for me. – *Letter 2*

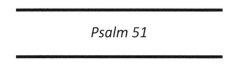

Psalm 51

Have you ever felt that something was amiss regarding your soul? Examining your conscience forces you to sit down, pray, and reflect on a real live list of ways in which you've repeatedly fallen short. Only then can God create in you a pure heart growing in holiness and thus, closer to Christ.

Day 6: Resigned to God's Will

AS FOR WHAT passes in me at present, I cannot express it. I have no pain or difficulty about my state because I have no will but that of God. I endeavor to accomplish His will in all things. And I am so resigned that I would not take up a straw from the ground against His order or from any motive but that of pure love for Him. – *Letter 2*

John 3:30; Matthew 16:24-26

To be always resigned to the will of God is one of the most beautiful traits of the Christian character and one of the most difficult to master. Unfortunately, we are so indoctrinated by the philosophy of the world that we tend to forget what following Christ is—thinking it's about us without any personal sacrifice. John the Baptist spent his whole life pointing people to Jesus. He was resolved in his mind and actions to increase Jesus, not himself. What areas of your life might you need to decrease in order that you may add more of Him each day until there's slowly but surely—and quite naturally—no room for yourself?

Day 7: Making it a Priority

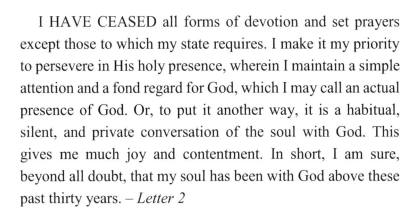

I HAVE CEASED all forms of devotion and set prayers except those to which my state requires. I make it my priority to persevere in His holy presence, wherein I maintain a simple attention and a fond regard for God, which I may call an actual presence of God. Or, to put it another way, it is a habitual, silent, and private conversation of the soul with God. This gives me much joy and contentment. In short, I am sure, beyond all doubt, that my soul has been with God above these past thirty years. – *Letter 2*

Luke 10:38-42

If you were to make a list of the top priorities in your life, what would it look like? As a Christ follower, we would all agree that God must be first. The question then is, *is He in fact first?* Our priorities, like Martha's, are often so full of the unnecessary. They control us and ruin our attitudes, leaving us distracted by small everyday things. As a result, like Martha, we miss the Lord speaking to us. Nothing is better than hearing the Lord speak, nothing is more important, nothing compares to that.

Day 8: Flaws and Weaknesses

YET, I THINK it is appropriate to tell you how I perceive myself before God, whom I behold as my King. I consider myself as the most wretched of men. I am full of faults, flaws, and weaknesses, and have committed all sorts of crimes against his King. Touched with a sensible regret I confess all my wickedness to Him. I ask His forgiveness. I abandon myself in His hands that He may do what He pleases with me.
– *Letter 2*

Romans 7:15-20; John 14:16-17

Paul describes the Christian experience as a constant battle between his spirit and his human nature. He wants to serve God wholeheartedly, but competing desires and priorities are constantly distracting and tripping him up. He doesn't pretend that by trying to do right he will earn God's favor and remove the struggle. And neither should we. Jesus is our only hope, and He alone has given us His Holy Spirit to guide us into all truth. Becoming sensitive to His leading makes all the difference and enables us to have victory over our old sinful nature.

Day 9: Goodness and Mercy

MY KING IS FULL OF MERCY and goodness. Far from chastising me, He embraces me with love. He makes me eat at His table. He serves me with His own hands and gives me the key to His treasures. He converses and delights Himself with me incessantly, in a thousand and a thousand ways. And He treats me in all respects as His favorite. In this way I consider myself continually in His holy presence. – *Letter 2*

Psalm 23:5-6

Perhaps your present situation feels difficult and overwhelming, and you wonder where God is in the midst of your trial. David paints a vivid picture of a loving God pursuing us in our most difficult times. He is not there to chastise us but rather to invite us to feast at His table and then honor us lavishly with His love. How blessed are we to have a God who is determined to chase after us until we finally know and experience the wonders of His goodness and mercy! Like David, our response should be one of worship and a desire to know Him all the more.

Day 10: Taste and See

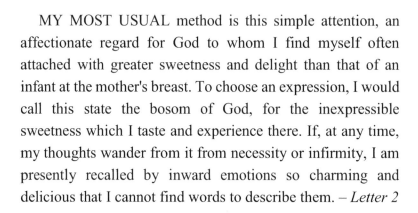

MY MOST USUAL method is this simple attention, an affectionate regard for God to whom I find myself often attached with greater sweetness and delight than that of an infant at the mother's breast. To choose an expression, I would call this state the bosom of God, for the inexpressible sweetness which I taste and experience there. If, at any time, my thoughts wander from it from necessity or infirmity, I am presently recalled by inward emotions so charming and delicious that I cannot find words to describe them. – *Letter 2*

Psalm 34:8; 1 Peter 2:1-3

To taste and see is experiential. You are being invited to try and experience the very nature of God. Have you done that? Do you take God at His Word? Have you experienced His goodness firsthand? Do you seek Him as your sole source of protection and realize that He loves you more than you can imagine? David is inviting you through this Psalm to put the matter to the test. Like David, once you have truly tasted and seen the goodness of God, your desire will be for others to experience what you have already come to know.

Day 11: Living Stones

AS FOR MY set hours of prayer, they are simply a continuation of the same exercise. Sometimes I consider myself as a stone before a carver, whereof He is to make a statue. Presenting myself thus before God, I desire Him to make His perfect image in my soul and render me entirely like Himself. – *Letter 2*

1 Peter 2:4-5

Once Brother Lawrence had tasted the kindness of the Lord, he imagined himself as a stone before a carver. He was a "living stone" being crafted in the image of the true Living Stone. As living stones, we are to find our value and identity by modeling the life of Jesus. Peter reminds us that God does not reject us, but rather sets us apart for His use. And part of that use is to offer spiritual sacrifices—our prayers, praises, will, bodies, time, and talents. Our willingness to sacrifice is an indication of our devotion to God. Do not reject being crafted into the image of the Living Stone! Allow your faith to empower your obedience because obedience is what pleases Him.

Day 12: He Knows Our Needs

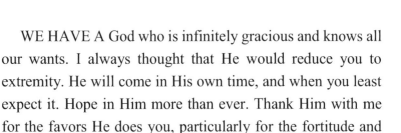

WE HAVE A God who is infinitely gracious and knows all our wants. I always thought that He would reduce you to extremity. He will come in His own time, and when you least expect it. Hope in Him more than ever. Thank Him with me for the favors He does you, particularly for the fortitude and patience which He gives you in your afflictions. It is a plain mark of the care He takes of you. Comfort yourself with Him and give thanks for all. – *Letter 3*

Matthew 6:25-34

Loving parents know what their children need, and they desire to fulfill those needs. In the same way, the God of the universe, who is also our loving Father, knows our needs even before we ask and is eager to meet those needs in much the same way that He feeds billions of birds each day. He knows us better than we know ourselves and wants us to be free from worrying about our needs. But if God already knows our needs, why do we need to ask Him to meet them? Theologian Soren Kierkegaard hints at the answer when he writes, "Prayer does not change God, but it changes him who prays."

Day 13: Pray Without Ceasing

A LITTLE LIFTING up of the heart and a remembrance of God suffices. One act of inward worship, though upon a march with sword in hand, are prayers which, however short, are nevertheless very acceptable to God. And, far from lessening a soldier's courage in occasions of danger, they actually serve to fortify it. Let him think of God as often as possible. Let him accustom himself, by degrees, to this small but holy exercise. No one sees it, and nothing is easier than to repeat these little internal adorations all through the day. – *Letter 3*

1 Thessalonians 5:16-18

Spending time with God is not relegated to a fraction of your waking hours. Brother Lawrence suggests a continuous, open-ended conversation with God throughout your day. Sounds impossible, right? Not really, it's all about shifting your thought process and talking with him about the common task of life. In other words, turning everyday moments into prayer. How would your day be different if every waking moment was lived with an awareness of God's active involvement in your thoughts and actions?

Day 14: Seeing What God Sees

HE OFTEN POINTS out our blindness and exclaims that those who content themselves with so little are to be pitied. God, says he, has infinite treasure to bestow, and we take so little through routine devotion which lasts but a moment. Blind as we are, we hinder God, and stop the current of His graces. But when He finds a soul penetrated with a lively faith, He pours into it His graces and favors plentifully. There they flow like a torrent, which, after being forcibly stopped against its ordinary course, when it has found a passage, spreads itself with impetuosity and abundance. – *Letter 4*

1 Corinthians 2:9-10

Sir Isaac Newton said, "As a blind man has no idea of colors, so have we no idea of the manner by which the all-wise God perceives and understands all things." This world has conditioned us to look at life according to its preferences and desires. Paul suggest there is an alternative way to look at our life—through the lens of how God thinks and through the ways and desires of God. This life discovery will add excitement and adventure like nothing we ever dreamed possible before.

Day 15: Spiritual Workout

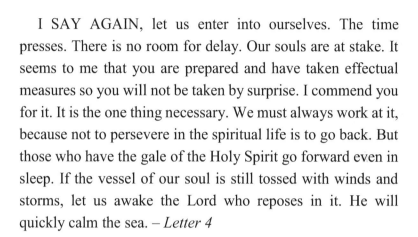

I SAY AGAIN, let us enter into ourselves. The time presses. There is no room for delay. Our souls are at stake. It seems to me that you are prepared and have taken effectual measures so you will not be taken by surprise. I commend you for it. It is the one thing necessary. We must always work at it, because not to persevere in the spiritual life is to go back. But those who have the gale of the Holy Spirit go forward even in sleep. If the vessel of our soul is still tossed with winds and storms, let us awake the Lord who reposes in it. He will quickly calm the sea. *– Letter 4*

Philippians 2:12-13

Our bodies tend to regress if we do not exercise on a regular basis. The same can be said for growing spiritually healthy. A spiritual workout is not just beneficial but a necessity. As a believer, God is your workout partner encouraging you to be persistent in working through the problems and trials and difficulties presented in ordinary daily life. Just as we benefit from a healthy body during our time on earth, staying spiritually fit offers benefits both now and for eternity.

Day 16: An Emptied Heart

I KNOW THAT for the right practice of it, the heart must be empty of all other things; because God will possess the heart alone. As He cannot possess it alone, without emptying it of all besides, so neither can He act there and do in it what He pleases unless it be left vacant to Him. *– Letter 5*

Matthew 19:16-30

Jesus tells us that the barrier to a more intimate relationship with Him is our unwillingness to empty our hearts of everything except Him. Surrendering things of earthly value does not come naturally to us. Our grip on this world is quite strong. But if we could empty our hearts of the desires of this world, we would realize that Jesus is inviting us to so much more. The rich young ruler missed this truth and left His encounter with Jesus sad when, instead, he could have left fulfilled and changed forever. Had he stayed and listened to what Jesus would say next, he would have heard what he would gain if he gave up everything he thought was important. What is your heart so consumed with that you cannot hear all that Christ wants to tell you?

Day 17: Never Lose Sight

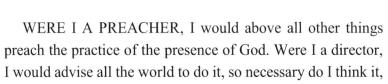

WERE I A PREACHER, I would above all other things preach the practice of the presence of God. Were I a director, I would advise all the world to do it, so necessary do I think it, and so easy too. Ah! Knew we but the want we have of the grace and assistance of God, we would never lose sight of Him, no, not for a moment.

Believe me. Immediately make a holy and firm resolution never more to forget Him. Resolve to spend the rest of your days in His sacred presence, deprived of all consolations for the love of Him if He thinks fit. Set heartily about this work, and if you do it sincerely, be assured that you will soon find the effects of it. – *Letter 5*

Deuteronomy 8:11-14

Often, when things are going well, it can be easy to lose sight of God's presence in our lives. Complacency is dangerous, so God warns us, that regardless of how well things are going, He still has more of Himself to give us. Do not buy into the illusion of self-sufficiency and forget that God is the source of every blessing you enjoy.

Day 18: The Center of Freedom

I CANNOT IMAGINE how religious persons can live satisfied without the practice of the presence of God. For my part I keep myself retired with Him in the depth and center of my soul as much as I can. While I am with Him, I fear nothing; but the least turning from Him is insupportable. – *Letter 6*

Luke 12:32

Brother Lawrence fears nothing when he remains in the center of God's will. Perhaps the opposite of fear is not courage but freedom—freedom of the soul. Free from being fearful, anxious, busy, distracted, stressed, and worried. Isn't this the freedom Christ says that we will experience if we will stay centered in His will? This centering does not absolve us from trials, temptations, and the normal struggles of life. However, this freedom that comes from centering ourselves in God brings with it joy, peace, and the ability to handle trouble of all kinds. If you lack this kind of freedom, ask God, and He will show you where you need to be. That is where freedom is found. Allow your mind and heart to stay in the center of God's will, despite how difficult it sometimes may be.

Day 19: Prone to Wander

WE MUST WORK faithfully without trouble or disquiet [anxiety], recalling our mind to God mildly and with tranquility as often as we find it wandering from Him. We must lay aside all other cares and even some forms of devotion, though very good in themselves, yet such as one often engages in routinely. Those devotions are only a means to attain to the end. Once we have established a habit of the practice of the presence of God, we are then with Him who is our end. We have no need to return to the means. *– Letter 6*

2 Corinthians 10:5

The verse *Prone to wander, Lord, I feel it, prone to leave the God I love* from the classic hymn *Come Thou Fount of Every Blessing* describes the wandering mind of most Christians. Brother Lawrence tells us that we should prepare to battle our own wandering thoughts, feelings, and habits, when attempting to permanently establish a continual conversation with God. It takes time and perseverance to make this spiritual exercise stick. A good start would be to take those wandering thoughts captive and try turning them into prayer.

Day 20: Nearer Than You Think

YOU NEED NOT CRY very loud. He is nearer to us than we are aware. And we do not always have to be in church to be with God. We may make an oratory (chapel) of our heart so we can, from time to time, retire to converse with Him in meekness, humility, and love. Everyone is capable of such familiar conversation with God, some more, some less. He knows what we can do. – *Letter 7*

Psalm 145:18-20; Matthew 28:20b

Nearness to God is a relative term. The fact is, God is as near to us as we would have Him be. Both Brother Lawrence and King David understood that God was with them not only in their corporate worship and quiet times, but all the time. When we made a commitment to follow Christ, He promised to be with us always. We may not always feel His presence, but we can be assured by faith He is there with us. Is He as close as you would have Him to be? If not, try walking in obedience to His Word without excuse or exception allowing yourself to be drawn into His truth. He will no doubt bless your obedience and draw near.

Day 21: To Live is Christ

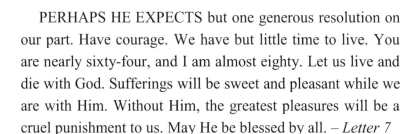

PERHAPS HE EXPECTS but one generous resolution on our part. Have courage. We have but little time to live. You are nearly sixty-four, and I am almost eighty. Let us live and die with God. Sufferings will be sweet and pleasant while we are with Him. Without Him, the greatest pleasures will be a cruel punishment to us. May He be blessed by all. – *Letter 7*

Philippians 1:21-22

What exactly does it mean to live and die with God? Brother Lawrence's chief desire in this life was to place Christ as the center point of his mind, heart, body and soul. As long as he lived, he would serve Christ, and when he died, he would get even more of Him in eternity. Likewise, the Apostle Paul discovered that a life lived for God becomes a life worth dying for—but he also understood that death was a good thing that moved him into the presence of God. Neither men were in a hurry to die since it was important to continue the work God gave them. But both were resolved to remain faithful to God in both life and death. That takes courage. Can your life be described as "to live is Christ, to die is gain?"

Day 22: Confessing our Faults

YOU ARE NOT the only one who is troubled with wandering thoughts. Our mind is extremely roving. But the will is mistress of all our faculties. She must recall our stray thoughts and carry them to God as their final end.

If the mind is not sufficiently controlled and disciplined at our first engaging in devotion, it contracts certain bad habits of wandering and dissipation. These are difficult to overcome. The mind can draw us, even against our will, to worldly things. I believe one remedy for this is to humbly confess our faults and beg God's mercy and help. – *Letter 8*

---

1 John 1:9-10

Brother Lawrence said that a genuine examination and confession of those areas in which we have done wrong is a remedy for a wandering heart. Our natural state is to deceive ourselves thinking we have no sin. Confession, however, is the alternative to denying sin and is a characteristic of a person who walks in the light. The cure for a wandering mind is to recognize in those moments just how horrendous your sin is before a holy God, and then confess it before Him.

Day 23: Too Many Words

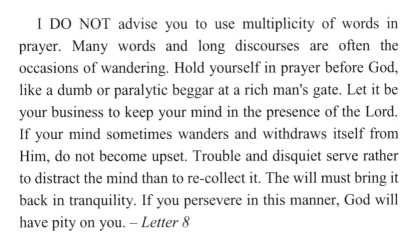

I DO NOT advise you to use multiplicity of words in prayer. Many words and long discourses are often the occasions of wandering. Hold yourself in prayer before God, like a dumb or paralytic beggar at a rich man's gate. Let it be your business to keep your mind in the presence of the Lord. If your mind sometimes wanders and withdraws itself from Him, do not become upset. Trouble and disquiet serve rather to distract the mind than to re-collect it. The will must bring it back in tranquility. If you persevere in this manner, God will have pity on you. – *Letter 8*

Matthew 6:7-8

Does your mind wandering during prayer? Brother Lawrence counsels us to not become discouraged when this happens as it only serves to further distract our minds leading us into using repetitious phrases and meaningless words that Jesus warned against. It's important to remember that God already knows what we need before we ask. With this understanding we can stop trying to move God with our words but rather present a heart that is motivated to do His will.

Day 24: Pleasing God

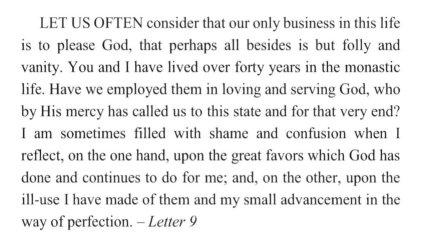

LET US OFTEN consider that our only business in this life is to please God, that perhaps all besides is but folly and vanity. You and I have lived over forty years in the monastic life. Have we employed them in loving and serving God, who by His mercy has called us to this state and for that very end? I am sometimes filled with shame and confusion when I reflect, on the one hand, upon the great favors which God has done and continues to do for me; and, on the other, upon the ill-use I have made of them and my small advancement in the way of perfection. – *Letter 9*

1 Thessalonians 2:4; Galatians 1:10

If we spend a great deal of time trying to please ourselves and others, then we leave no room for trying to please God. Paul tells us that the purpose of our faith is to please God, not other people. Learning to please God and sensing His approval is a higher calling and is much more fulfilling. It's what we were created to do! When we turn our thoughts and actions from pleasing others to pleasing Christ, that's when we will find contentment, peace, and freedom.

Day 25: Seize the Day

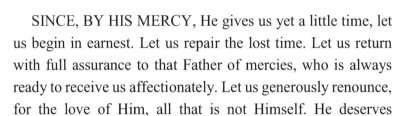

SINCE, BY HIS MERCY, He gives us yet a little time, let us begin in earnest. Let us repair the lost time. Let us return with full assurance to that Father of mercies, who is always ready to receive us affectionately. Let us generously renounce, for the love of Him, all that is not Himself. He deserves infinitely more. Let us think of Him perpetually. Let us put all our trust in Him. – *Letter 9*

Hebrews 3:13; Ephesians 5:15-16

The Latin phrase *Carpe diem* or "seize the day" is used to express the idea that one should enjoy life while one can. Brother Lawrence might claim that "seizing the day" is actually a biblical concept and rightfully so in that our time on this earth is limited, so what we do with it should be of the upmost importance. What will you do with the time you are given? Will you spend it frivolously pursuing the things of the world or seizing every opportunity God gives to invest in His purposes "as long as it is called 'Today?'" We can never get back the time we wasted outside of God's purpose, but we can redeem it by investing the time we have left in what matters.

Day 26: Immeasurably More

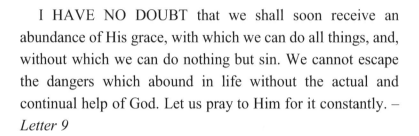

I HAVE NO DOUBT that we shall soon receive an abundance of His grace, with which we can do all things, and, without which we can do nothing but sin. We cannot escape the dangers which abound in life without the actual and continual help of God. Let us pray to Him for it constantly. – *Letter 9*

Ephesians 3:20-21

How good is your imagination? God's power is greater than that! Paul tells us that God can "do immeasurably more than all we ask or imagine." God has plans far above anything we can dream up and desires that we join Him in His plans. Too often though, we limit our expectations based on our own power or what we perceive will happen. We need to stop living in our own strength and instead rely wholly on His. God is not there to grant every wish we have but rather to provide us "an abundance of His grace" as we faithfully lean into His love, power, and guidance. Don't limit God's activity in your life to what you think is best. Be open to letting Him work fully even when you do not understand.

Day 27: Knowing God

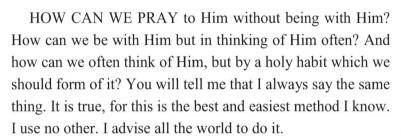

HOW CAN WE PRAY to Him without being with Him? How can we be with Him but in thinking of Him often? And how can we often think of Him, but by a holy habit which we should form of it? You will tell me that I always say the same thing. It is true, for this is the best and easiest method I know. I use no other. I advise all the world to do it.

We must know before we can love. In order to know God, we must often think of Him. And when we come to love Him, we shall then also think of Him often, for our heart will be with our treasure. *– Letter 9*

1 John 4:8

Your ability to love and trust someone is directly related to how well you know them. Brother Lawrence reasoned that before we can love and trust God, we must know Him, and to know Him, we must think of Him often. Since we were made in God's image and He is love, then knowing God better should help us better understand ourselves and in turn love others. But knowing someone on a deeper level takes time and opportunity. Do you think of Him often?

Day 28: Neglecting God

PLEASE KEEP MY recommendation in mind that you think of God often; by day, by night, in your business, and even in your diversions. He is always near you and with you. Leave Him not alone. You would think it rude to leave a friend alone who came to visit you. Why, then, must God be neglected? Do not forget Him but think on Him often. Adore Him continually. Live and die with Him. This is the glorious work of a Christian; in a word, this is our profession. If we do not know it, we must learn it. – *Letter 10*

Isaiah 43:22

We are all guilty of neglecting God. Instead, we choose to spend time flipping channels, surfing the web, or swiping through endless social media posts rather than reading our Bibles or spending time in prayer. Isaiah tells us that Israel had also ceased crying out to God. They begin to think of God as a burden upon their lives, so they became weary of Him and suffered as a result. Make a conscious decision today to turn your focus back to Jesus and make Him a priority in your life, and there you will once again discover the joy of the Lord.

Day 29: Strength to Endure

I DO NOT PRAY that you may be delivered from your pains; but I pray earnestly that God gives you strength and patience to bear them as long as He pleases. Comfort yourself with Him who holds you fastened to the cross. He will loose you when He thinks fit. Happy are those who suffer with Him. Accustom yourself to suffer in that manner and seek from Him the strength to endure as much, and as long, as He judges necessary for you. – *Letter 11*

Romans 5:3-5

In this life we will experience tragedy, heartache, hurt, and pain. How is it possible to rejoice in that? Paul's exhortation to rejoice is not to rejoice because we are suffering, but rather to rejoice in our suffering. Suffering comes to us all, but there is hope in it. It's only during those difficult times that you discover whether you've placed your hope in Jesus or something else. Brother Lawrence prayed for the patience to endure his suffering. When we endure, a God-forged character is formed, and even in the worst of times, that is when those who are suffering without hope often sit up and take notice.

Day 30: A Place at the Table

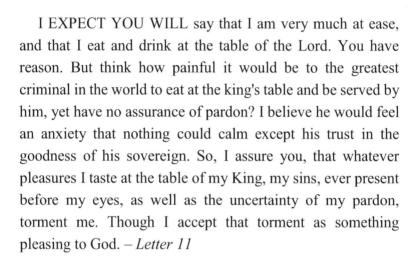

I EXPECT YOU WILL say that I am very much at ease, and that I eat and drink at the table of the Lord. You have reason. But think how painful it would be to the greatest criminal in the world to eat at the king's table and be served by him, yet have no assurance of pardon? I believe he would feel an anxiety that nothing could calm except his trust in the goodness of his sovereign. So, I assure you, that whatever pleasures I taste at the table of my King, my sins, ever present before my eyes, as well as the uncertainty of my pardon, torment me. Though I accept that torment as something pleasing to God. *– Letter 11*

2 Samuel 9:13

Mephibosheth had everything to fear being the disabled grandson of Saul, King David's enemy. Yet David's promise to Mephibosheth to always have a seat at his table is a beautiful picture of the invitation God gives to us. We are weak and broken, yet God has a place for us at His table regardless of our flaws and shortcomings. Though we are not worthy, He welcomes us as one of His own sons.

Day 31: Suffering for His Sake

BE SATISFIED WITH the condition in which God places you. However happy you may think me, I envy you. Pain and suffering would be a paradise to me, if I could suffer with my God. The greatest pleasures would be hell if I relished them without Him. My only consolation would be to suffer something for His sake. – *Letter 11*

1 Peter 4:12-13

Suffering is not something that we naturally seek out. More often we try to avoid it at all costs. But Peter tells us not to be surprised when anyone who follows Jesus wholeheartedly experiences difficulty. We will all experience suffering, often as a result of trying to follow the teachings of Christ in a world that rebels against Him. Brother Lawrence considered it an honor to suffer for Christ. He knew that his suffering would either make or break his faith, and he relished the opportunity to become more like Christ. When we suffer for the sake of Christ, it helps mature our faith as we become more like Him. Fully devoted Christians can rejoice in suffering because we know that it only makes our faith stronger.

Day 32: Spiritual Sight

I MUST, IN A LITTLE TIME, go to God. What comforts me in this life is that I now see Him by faith. I see Him in such a manner that I sometimes say, I believe no more, but I see. I feel what faith teaches us, and, in that assurance and that practice of faith, I live and die with Him. – *Letter 11*

Ephesians 1:18

The Apostles could accurately teach about Jesus because they were personal eyewitnesses to his ministry on earth. Although Brother Lawrence was never in the physical presence of Jesus, he cultivated a lifestyle of seeing where God was at work around him and then joining Him there. This spiritual insight allowed him to see from God's perspective. There is an old adage that goes, "those who leave everything in God's hand will eventually see God's hand in everything." If you are having difficulty seeing God, try to quiet yourself, wait, and ask the Holy Spirit for the spiritual insight to see what God is doing around you. Then you will begin to see yourself, your problems, and your past, present, and future a little clearer the closer you get to God.

Day 33: Living Sacrifice

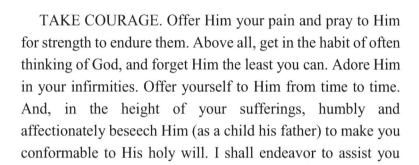

TAKE COURAGE. Offer Him your pain and pray to Him for strength to endure them. Above all, get in the habit of often thinking of God, and forget Him the least you can. Adore Him in your infirmities. Offer yourself to Him from time to time. And, in the height of your sufferings, humbly and affectionately beseech Him (as a child his father) to make you conformable to His holy will. I shall endeavor to assist you with my poor prayers. *– Letter 12*

Romans 12:1

Brother Lawrence saw every moment of every day as an opportunity to offer himself to his Savior. He willingly surrendered himself and his own interests for his love of Christ and his desire to serve Him and his fellow man. Paul tells us that to be a "living sacrifice" means that we continually offer ourselves for the Lord's glory. Paul was not talking about just our physical bodies but our entire being. A life that is completely dedicated to Jesus Christ is the kind of worship that God desires from us. What's keeping you from living this kind of life? What can you do to remove those barriers?

Day 34: Unspeakable Joy

GOD HAS MANY WAYS of drawing us to Himself. He sometimes seems to hide Himself from us. But faith alone ought to be our support. Faith is the foundation of our confidence. We must put all our faith in God. He will not fail us in time of need. I do not know how God will dispose of me, but I am always happy. All the world suffers and I, who deserve the severest discipline, feel joys so continual and great that I can scarcely contain them. – *Letter 12*

1 Peter 1:8-9

The King James translation uses the phrase "joy unspeakable." Imagine a joy so incredible that it cannot be fully described. A joy that cannot be attached to anything in this world—not to your spouse, job, children, or possessions— which may bring you happiness and pleasure but is ultimately dependent on circumstances. Since we cannot completely control our circumstances, we will constantly be disappointed. We can, however, rejoice knowing there's a supernatural joy available to us in Christ, not dependent on circumstance but on the mighty power and love of God.

Day 35: Wretched Man

I WOULD WILLINGLY ASK God for a part of your sufferings. I know my weakness is so great that if He left me one moment to myself, I would be the most wretched man alive. And yet, I do not know how He could leave me alone because faith gives me as strong a conviction as reason. He never forsakes us until we have first forsaken Him. Let us fear to leave Him. Let us always be with Him. Let us live and die in His presence. *– Letter 12*

Romans 7:24-25

Brother Lawrence was honest about his weakness apart from Christ. He recognized the internal battle within himself to do wrong: that in his own strength, he could not do right simply by determining to do so. As believers, we all understand the frustration, confusion, and doubt caused by our sin. Even though we've been set free from our sin, we do not always live into that reality. Struggling against sin is a lifelong battle. However, it's won each day as we submit ourselves to the Spirit of God resting in His power to deliver us from our own weaknesses.

Day 36: Boast in God

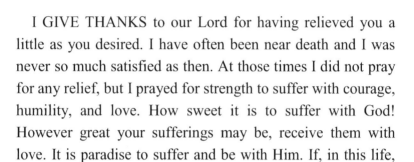

I GIVE THANKS to our Lord for having relieved you a little as you desired. I have often been near death and I was never so much satisfied as then. At those times I did not pray for any relief, but I prayed for strength to suffer with courage, humility, and love. How sweet it is to suffer with God! However great your sufferings may be, receive them with love. It is paradise to suffer and be with Him. If, in this life, we might enjoy the peace of paradise, we must accustom ourselves to a familiar, humble, and affectionate conversation with God. – *Letter 14*

---

2 Corinthians 12:9

Brother Lawrence did not hesitate to boast about the powerful presence of the Holy Spirit in his life as he neared death. It was during those times of suffering that he discovered an even deeper connection with his Creator who sufficiently made up for any of his weakness. We should not deny our weaknesses as they are the very things that lead us to God in the first place. Embracing our weakness allows for more of the Lord's power and grace to shine through us.

Day 37: Filling Our Minds

WE MUST HINDER our spirits wandering from Him on all occasions. We must make our heart a spiritual temple so we can constantly adore Him. We must continually watch over ourselves so we do not do anything that may displease Him. When our minds and hearts are filled with God, suffering becomes full of unction and consolation. *– Letter 14*

Romans 12:2

Conforming to this world requires little effort. It's easy: just do what everyone else does around you. As a believer we need to replace our old unhealthy thought patterns with new ones modeled after the life of Christ. When you are struggling with actions that are in conflict with your faith, pray and ask God to transform your mind. Allowing God access to all of our thoughts will transform you into a reflection of what He wants you to be. Transforming the mind requires more effort than simply not following the patterns of this world. It happens as we intentionally expose ourselves to a daily intake of God's Word. If you want to live differently, you must begin to think differently and adopt different habits.

Day 38: Keep on Knocking

I WELL KNOW that to arrive at this state, the beginning is very difficult because we must act purely on faith. But though it is difficult, we know also that we can do all things with the grace of God. He never refuses those who ask earnestly. Knock. Persevere in knocking. And I answer for it, that, in His due time, He will open His graces to you. He will grant, all at once, what He has deferred during many years. – *Letter 14*

Matthew 7:7-8

Brother Lawrence believes that the most powerful thing a Christian can do is pray. Yet how often do we give up on prayer when we don't immediately receive an answer? Jesus invites us to bring all of our requests to God, but His message is clear—persevere in your praying despite obstacles or difficulties. Our perseverance in prayer is designed to help us discover God's will as we learn to focus on the Lord's faithfulness rather than our circumstances. What have you been seeking God about? What doors are you asking Him to open? Keep on asking. Keep on seeking. Keep on knocking.

Day 39: Working for the Good

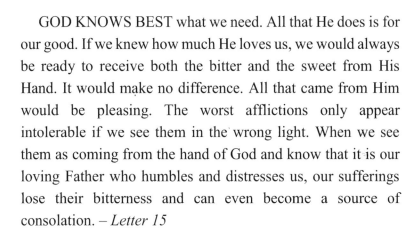

GOD KNOWS BEST what we need. All that He does is for our good. If we knew how much He loves us, we would always be ready to receive both the bitter and the sweet from His Hand. It would make no difference. All that came from Him would be pleasing. The worst afflictions only appear intolerable if we see them in the wrong light. When we see them as coming from the hand of God and know that it is our loving Father who humbles and distresses us, our sufferings lose their bitterness and can even become a source of consolation. – *Letter 15*

Romans 8:28

The Apostle Paul does not say that all things that happen to us are good. Some things and events are decidedly bad. But God does work all things together for His good and our good. How would our perspective on life change if we viewed both the good and the bad as somehow working together by God's design for our ultimate well-being. Even in the things we do not understand, He is always with us, working out His good purpose in every circumstance.

Day 40: A Change of Heart

ARE WE NOT RUDE and deserve blame if we leave Him alone to busy ourselves with trifles which do not please Him and perhaps even offend Him? These trifles may one day cost us dearly. Let us begin earnestly to be devoted to Him. Let us cast everything else out of our hearts. He wants to possess the heart alone. Beg this favor of Him. If we do all we can, we will soon see that change wrought in us which we so greatly desire.
– Letter 15

Psalm 51:10

In his brokenness, King David humbly cried out to God to create in him a clean heart and a renewed spirit. At some point in your walk you might have found yourself praying a similar prayer. Brother Lawrence tells us that God "wants to possess the heart alone." But this can only happen when we let down our guard, honestly examine our own heart, and recognize our need for Christ. Both David and Brother Lawrence realized that nothing can compare with the joy that comes from a pure heart and walking with God. Has God created in you a clean heart that desires to please Him?

The Practice of the Presence of God

Preface

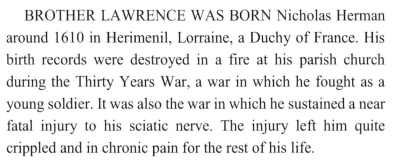

BROTHER LAWRENCE WAS BORN Nicholas Herman around 1610 in Herimenil, Lorraine, a Duchy of France. His birth records were destroyed in a fire at his parish church during the Thirty Years War, a war in which he fought as a young soldier. It was also the war in which he sustained a near fatal injury to his sciatic nerve. The injury left him quite crippled and in chronic pain for the rest of his life.

The details of his early life are few and sketchy. However, we know he was educated both at home and by his parish priest whose first name was Lawrence and who was greatly admired by the young Nicolas. He was well read and, from an early age, drawn to a spiritual life of faith and love for God.

We also know that in the years between the abrupt end of his duties as a soldier and his entry into monastic life, he spent a period of time in the wilderness living like one of the early desert fathers. Also, prior to entering the monastery, and perhaps as preparation, he spent time as a civil servant. In his characteristic, self-deprecating way, he mentions that he was a "footman who was clumsy and broke everything".

At mid-life he entered a newly established monastery in Paris where he became the cook for the community which grew to over one hundred members. After fifteen years, his duties were shifted to the sandal repair shop but, even then, he often returned to the busy kitchen to help out.

In times as troubled as today, Brother Lawrence, discovered, then followed, a pure and uncomplicated way to walk continually in God's presence. For some forty years, he lived and walked with Our Father at his side. Yet, through his own words, we learn that Brother Lawrence's first ten years were full of severe trials and challenges.

A gentle man of joyful spirit, Brother Lawrence shunned attention and the limelight, knowing that outside distraction "spoils all". It was not until after his death that a few of his letters were collected. Joseph de Beaufort, representative and counsel to the local archbishop, first published the letters in a small pamphlet. The following year, in a second publication which he titled, 'The Practice of the Presence of God', de Beaufort included, as introductory material, the content of four conversations he had with Brother Lawrence.

In this small book, through letters and conversations, Brother Lawrence simply and beautifully explains how to continually walk with God - not from the head but from the heart. Brother Lawrence left the gift of a way of life available to anyone who seeks to know God's peace and presence; that anyone, regardless of age or circumstance, can practice - anywhere, anytime. Brother Lawrence also left the gift of a direct approach to living in God's presence that is as practical today as it was three hundred years ago.

Brother Lawrence died in 1691, having practiced God's presence for over forty years. His quiet death was much like his monastic life where each day and each hour was a new beginning and a fresh commitment to love God with all his heart.

Conversations: Introduction

INTRODUCTION: AT THE TIME of de Beaufort's interviews, Brother Lawrence was in his late fifties. Joseph de Beaufort later commented that the crippled brother, who was then in charge of the upkeep of over one hundred pairs of sandals, was "rough in appearance but gentle in grace".

First Conversation

THE FIRST TIME I SAW Brother Lawrence was upon the 3rd of August 1666. He told me that God had done him a singular favor in his conversion at the age of eighteen. During that winter, upon seeing a tree stripped of its leaves and considering that within a little time the leaves would be renewed and after that the flowers and fruit appear, Brother Lawrence received a high view of the Providence and Power of God which has never since been effaced from his soul. This view had perfectly set him loose from the world and kindled in him such a love for God, that he could not tell whether it had increased in the forty years that he had lived since.

Brother Lawrence said he had been footman to M. Fieubert, the treasurer, and that he was a great awkward fellow who broke everything. He finally decided to enter a monastery thinking that he would there be made to smart for his awkwardness and the faults he would commit, and so he would sacrifice his life with its pleasures to God. But Brother Lawrence said that God had surprised him because he met with nothing but satisfaction in that state.

Brother Lawrence related that we should establish ourselves in a sense of God's Presence by continually conversing with Him. It was a shameful thing to quit His conversation to think of trifles and fooleries. We should feed and nourish our souls with high notions of God which would yield us great joy in being devoted to Him.

He said we ought to quicken and enliven our faith. It was lamentable we had so little. Instead of taking faith for the rule of their conduct, men amused themselves with trivial devotions which changed daily. He said that faith was sufficient to bring us to a high degree of perfection. We ought to give ourselves up to God with regard both to things temporal and spiritual and seek our satisfaction only in the fulfilling of His will. Whether God led us by suffering or by consolation all would be equal to a soul truly resigned.

He said we need fidelity in those disruptions in the ebb and flow of prayer when God tries our love to Him. This was the time for a complete act of resignation, whereof one act alone could greatly promote our spiritual advancement.

He said that as far as the miseries and sins he heard of daily in the world, he was so far from wondering at them, that, on the contrary, he was surprised there were not more considering the malice sinners were capable of. For his part, he prayed for them. But knowing that God could remedy the mischief they did when He pleased, he gave himself no further trouble.

Brother Lawrence said to arrive at such resignation as God requires, we should carefully watch over all the passions that mingle in spiritual as well as temporal things. God would give light concerning those passions to those who truly desire to serve Him.

At the end of this first conversation Brother Lawrence said that if my purpose for the visit was to sincerely discuss how to serve God, I might come to him as often as I pleased and without any fear of being troublesome. If this was not the case, then I ought visit him no more.

Second Conversation

BROTHER LAWRENCE TOLD ME he had always been governed by love without selfish views. Since he resolved to make the love of God the end of all his actions, he had found reasons to be well satisfied with his method. He was pleased when he could take up a straw from the ground for the love of God, seeking Him only, and nothing else, not even His gifts.

He said he had been long troubled in mind from a certain belief that he should be damned. All the men in the world could not have persuaded him to the contrary. This trouble of mind had lasted four years during which time he had suffered much.

Finally, he reasoned: I did not engage in a religious life but for the love of God. I have endeavored to act only for Him. Whatever becomes of me, whether I be lost or saved, I will always continue to act purely for the love of God. I shall have this good at least that till death I shall have done all that is in me to love Him. From that time on Brother Lawrence lived his life in perfect liberty and continual joy. He placed his sins between himself and God to tell Him that he did not deserve His favors, yet God still continued to bestow them in abundance.

Brother Lawrence said that in order to form a habit of conversing with God continually and referring all we do to Him, we must at first apply to Him with some diligence. Then, after a little care, we would find His love inwardly excite us to it without any difficulty.

He expected after the pleasant days God had given him, he would have his turn of pain and suffering. Yet he was not uneasy about it. Knowing that, since he could do nothing of himself, God would not fail to give him the strength to bear them.

When an occasion of practicing some virtue was offered, he addressed himself to God saying, "Lord, I cannot do this unless Thou enablest me". And then he received strength more than sufficient. When he had failed in his duty, he only confessed his fault saying to God, "I shall never do otherwise, if You leave me to myself. It is You who must hinder my falling and mend what is amiss." Then, after this, he gave himself no further uneasiness about it.

Brother Lawrence said we ought to act with God in the greatest simplicity, speaking to Him frankly and plainly, and imploring His assistance in our affairs just as they happen. God never failed to grant it, as Brother Lawrence had often experienced.

He said he had been lately sent into Burgundy to buy the provision of wine for the community. This was a very unwelcome task for him because he had no turn for business and because he was lame and could not go about the boat but by rolling himself over the casks. Yet he gave himself no uneasiness about it, nor about the purchase of the wine. He said to God, it was His business he was about, and that he afterwards found it very well performed. He mentioned that it had turned out the same way the year before when he was sent to Auvergne.

So, likewise, in his business in the kitchen (to which he had naturally a great aversion), having accustomed himself to do everything there for the love of God and asking for His grace to do his work well, he had found everything easy during the fifteen years that he had been employed there. He was very pleased with the post he was now in. Yet he was as ready to quit that as the former, since he tried to please God by doing little things for the love of Him in any work he did. With him the set times of prayer were not different from other times. He retired to pray according to the directions of his superior, but he did not need such retirement nor ask for it because his greatest business did not divert him from God.

Since he knew his obligation to love God in all things, and as he endeavored to do so, he had no need of a director to advise him, but he greatly needed a confessor to absolve him. He said he was very sensible of his faults but not discouraged by them. He confessed them to God and made no excuses. Then, he peaceably resumed his usual practice of love and adoration.

In his trouble of mind, Brother Lawrence had consulted no one. Knowing only by the light of faith that God was present, he contented himself with directing all his actions to Him. He did everything with a desire to please Him and let what would come of it.

He said that useless thoughts spoil all - that the mischief began there. We ought to reject them as soon as we perceived their impertinence and return to our communion with God. In the beginning he had often passed his time appointed for prayer in rejecting wandering thoughts and falling right back into them. He could never regulate his devotion by certain methods as some do. Nevertheless, at first he had meditated for some time, but afterwards that went off in a manner that he could give no account of. Brother Lawrence emphasized that all bodily mortifications and other exercises are useless unless they serve to arrive at the union with God by love. He had well considered this. He found that the shortest way to go straight to God was by a continual exercise of love and doing all things for His sake.

He noted that there was a great difference between the acts of the intellect and those of the will. Acts of the intellect were comparatively of little value. Acts of the will were all important. Our only business was to love and delight ourselves in God. All possible kinds of mortification, if they were void of the love of God, could not efface a single sin. Instead, we ought, without anxiety, to expect the pardon of our sins from the blood of Jesus Christ only endeavoring to love Him with all our hearts. And he noted that God seemed to have granted the greatest favors to the greatest sinners as more signal monuments of His mercy.

Brother Lawrence said the greatest pains or pleasures of this world were not to be compared with what he had experienced of both kinds in a spiritual state. As a result, he feared nothing, desiring only one thing of God - that he might not offend Him. He said he carried no guilt. "When I fail in my duty, I readily acknowledge it, saying, I am used to do so. I shall never do otherwise if I am left to myself. If I fail not, then I give God thanks acknowledging that it comes from Him."

Third Conversation

BROTHER LAWRENCE TOLD ME that the foundation of the spiritual life in him had been a high notion and esteem of God in faith. When he had once well established his faith he had no other care but to reject every other thought so he might perform all his actions for the love of God. He said when sometimes he had not thought of God for a good while he did not disquiet himself for it. Having acknowledged his wretchedness to God, he simply returned to Him with so much the greater trust in Him.

He said the trust we put in God honors Him much and draws down great graces. Also, that it was impossible not only that God should deceive but that He should long let a soul suffer which is perfectly resigned to Him and resolved to endure everything for His sake.

Brother Lawrence often experienced the ready succors of Divine Grace. And because of his experience of grace, when he had business to do, he did not think of it beforehand. When it was time to do it, he found in God, as in a clear mirror, all that was fit for him to do. When outward business diverted him a little from the thought of God a fresh remembrance coming from God invested his soul and so inflamed and transported him that it was difficult for him to contain himself. He said he was more united to God in his outward employments than when he left them for devotion in retirement.

Brother Lawrence said that the worst that could happen to him was to lose that sense of God which he had enjoyed so long. Yet the goodness of God assured him He would not forsake him utterly and that He would give him strength to bear whatever evil He permitted to happen to him. Brother Lawrence, therefore, said he feared nothing. He had no occasion to consult with anybody about his state. In the past, when he had attempted to do it, he had always come away more perplexed. Since Brother Lawrence was ready to lay down his life for the love of God, he had no apprehension of danger.

He said that perfect resignation to God was a sure way to heaven, a way in which we have always sufficient light for our conduct. In the beginning of the spiritual life we ought to be faithful in doing our duty and denying ourselves and then, after a time, unspeakable pleasures followed. In difficulties we need only have recourse to Jesus Christ and beg His grace with which everything became easy.

Brother Lawrence said that many do not advance in the Christian progress because they stick in penances and particular exercises while they neglect the love of God which is the end. This appeared plainly by their works and was the reason why we see so little solid virtue. He said there needed neither art nor science for going to God, but only a heart resolutely determined to apply itself to nothing but Him and to love Him only.

Fourth Conversation

BROTHER LAWRENCE SPOKE WITH great openness of heart concerning his manner of going to God whereof some part is related already. He told me that all consists in one hearty renunciation of everything which we are sensible does not lead to God. We might accustom ourselves to a continual conversation with Him with freedom and in simplicity. We need only to recognize God intimately present with us and address ourselves to Him every moment. We need to beg His assistance for knowing His will in things doubtful and for rightly performing those which we plainly see He requires of us, offering them to Him before we do them, and giving Him thanks when we have completed them.

In our conversation with God we should also engage in praising, adoring, and loving Him incessantly for His infinite goodness and perfection. Without being discouraged on account of our sins, we should pray for His grace with a perfect confidence, as relying upon the infinite merits of our Lord. Brother Lawrence said that God never failed offering us His grace at each action. It never failed except when Brother Lawrence's thoughts had wandered from a sense of God's Presence, or he forgot to ask His assistance. He said that God always gave us light in our doubts, when we had no other design but to please Him.

Our sanctification did not depend upon changing our

works. Instead, it depended on doing that for God's sake which we commonly do for our own. He thought it was lamentable to see how many people mistook the means for the end, addicting themselves to certain works which they performed very imperfectly by reason of their human or selfish regards. The most excellent method he had found for going to God was that of doing our common business without any view of pleasing men but purely for the love of God.

Brother Lawrence felt it was a great delusion to think that the times of prayer ought to differ from other times. We are as strictly obliged to adhere to God by action in the time of action, as by prayer in its season. His own prayer was nothing else but a sense of the presence of God, his soul being at that time insensible to everything but Divine Love. When the appointed times of prayer were past, he found no difference, because he still continued with God, praising and blessing Him with all his might. Thus he passed his life in continual joy. Yet he hoped that God would give him somewhat to suffer when he grew stronger.

Brother Lawrence said we ought, once and for all, heartily put our whole trust in God, and make a total surrender of ourselves to Him, secure that He would not deceive us. We ought not weary of doing little things for the love of God, who regards not the greatness of the work, but the love with which it is performed. We should not wonder if, in the beginning, we often failed in our endeavors, but that at last we should gain a habit which will naturally produce its acts in us without our care and to our exceeding great delight.

The whole substance of religion was faith, hope, and

charity. In the practice of these we become united to the will of God. Everything else is indifferent and to be used as a means that we may arrive at our end and then be swallowed up by faith and charity. All things are possible to him who believes. They are less difficult to him who hopes. They are more easy to him who loves, and still more easy to him who perseveres in the practice of these three virtues. The end we ought to propose to ourselves is to become, in this life, the most perfect worshippers of God we can possibly be, and as we hope to be through all eternity.

We must, from time to time, honestly consider and thoroughly examine ourselves. We will, then, realize that we are worthy of great contempt. Brother Lawrence noted that when we directly confront ourselves in this manner, we will understand why we are subject to all kinds of misery and problems. We will realize why we are subject to changes and fluctuations in our health, mental outlook, and dispositions. And we will, indeed, recognize that we deserve all the pain and labors God sends to humble us.

After this, we should not wonder that troubles, temptations, oppositions, and contradictions happen to us from men. We ought, on the contrary, to submit ourselves to them and bear them as long as God pleases as things highly advantageous to us. The greater perfection a soul aspires after, the more dependent it is upon Divine Grace.

Being questioned by one of his own community (to whom he was obliged to open himself) by what means he had attained such an habitual sense of God, Brother Lawrence told him that, since his first coming to the monastery, he had considered God as the end of all his thoughts and desires, as the mark to which they should tend, and in which they should terminate.

He noted that in the beginning of his novitiate he spent the hours appointed for private prayer in thinking of God so as to convince his mind and impress deeply upon his heart the Divine existence. He did this by devout sentiments and submission to the lights of faith, rather than by studied reasonings and elaborate meditations. By this short and sure method he exercised himself in the knowledge and love of God, resolving to use his utmost endeavor to live in a continual sense of His Presence, and, if possible, never to forget Him more.

When he had thus, in prayer, filled his mind with great sentiments of that Infinite Being, he went to his work appointed in the kitchen (for he was then cook for the community). There having first considered severally the things his office required, and when and how each thing was to be done, he spent all the intervals of his time, both before and after his work, in prayer.

When he began his business, he said to God with a filial trust in Him, "O my God, since Thou art with me, and I must now, in obedience to Thy commands, apply my mind to these outward things, I beseech Thee to grant me the grace to continue in Thy Presence; and to this end do Thou prosper me with Thy assistance. Receive all my works and possess all my affections." As he proceeded in his work, he continued his familiar conversation with his Maker, imploring His grace, and offering to Him all his actions.

When he had finished, he examined himself how he had

discharged his duty. If he found well, he returned thanks to God. If otherwise, he asked pardon and, without being discouraged, he set his mind right again. He then continued his exercise of the presence of God as if he had never deviated from it. "Thus," said he, "by rising after my falls, and by frequently renewed acts of faith and love, I am come to a state wherein it would be as difficult for me not to think of God as it was at first to accustom myself to it."

As Brother Lawrence had found such an advantage in walking in the presence of God, it was natural for him to recommend it earnestly to others. More strikingly, his example was a stronger inducement than any arguments he could propose. His very countenance was edifying with such a sweet and calm devotion appearing that he could not but affect the beholders.

It was observed, that in the greatest hurry of business in the kitchen, he still preserved his recollection and heavenly-mindedness. He was never hasty nor loitering but did each thing in its season with an even uninterrupted composure and tranquility of spirit. "The time of business," said he, "does not with me differ from the time of prayer. In the noise and clutter of my kitchen, while several persons are at the same time calling for different things, I possess God in as great tranquility as if I were upon my knees at the Blessed Supper."

Letters: Introduction

BROTHER LAWRENCE'S LETTERS ARE the very heart and soul of what is titled 'The Practice of the Presence of God'. All of these letters were written during the last ten years of his life. Many of them were to long-time friends, a Carmelite sister and a sister at a nearby convent. One or both of these friends were from his native village, perhaps relatives.

The first letter was probably written to the prioress of one of these convents. The second letter was written to Brother Lawrence's own spiritual adviser. Note that the fourth letter is written in the third person where Brother Lawrence describes his own experience. The letters follow the tradition of substituting M— for specific names.

First Letter

YOU SO EARNESTLY DESIRE that I describe the method by which I arrived at that habitual sense of God's presence, which our merciful Lord has been pleased to grant me. I am complying with your request with my request that you show my letter to no one. If I knew that you would let it be seen, all the desire I have for your spiritual progress would not be enough to make me comply.

The account I can give you is: Having found in many books different methods of going to God and divers practices of the spiritual life, I thought this would serve rather to puzzle me than facilitate what I sought after, which was nothing but how to become wholly God's. This made me resolve to give the all for the All. After having given myself wholly to God, to make all the satisfaction I could for my sins, I renounced, for the love of Him, everything that was not He, and I began to live as if there was none but He and I in the world.

Sometimes I considered myself before Him as a poor criminal at the feet of his judge. At other times I beheld Him in my heart as my Father, as my God. I worshipped Him the oftenest I could, keeping my mind in His holy presence and recalling it as often as I found it wandered from Him. I made this my business, not only at the appointed times of prayer but all the time; every hour, every minute, even in the height of my work, I drove from my mind everything that interrupted my thoughts of God.

I found no small pain in this exercise. Yet I continued it, notwithstanding all the difficulties that occurred. And I tried not to trouble or disquiet myself when my mind wandered. Such has been my common practice ever since I entered religious life. Though I have done it very imperfectly, I have found great advantages by it. These, I well know, are to be imputed to the mercy and goodness of God because we can do nothing without Him; and I still less than any.

When we are faithful to keep ourselves in His holy presence, and set Him always before us, this hinders our offending Him, and doing anything that may displease Him. It also begets in us a holy freedom, and, if I may so speak, a familiarity with God, where, when we ask, He supplies the graces we need. Over time, by often repeating these acts, they become habitual, and the presence of God becomes quite natural to us.

Please give Him thanks with me, for His great goodness towards me, which I can never sufficiently express, and for the many favors He has done to so miserable a sinner as I am. May all things praise Him. Amen.

Second Letter

NOT FINDING MY MANNER OF LIFE described in books, although I have no problem with that, yet, for reassurance, I would appreciate your thoughts about it.

In conversation some days ago a devout person told me the spiritual life was a life of grace, which begins with servile fear, which is increased by hope of eternal life, and which is consummated by pure love; that each of these states had its different steps, by which one arrives at last at that blessed consummation.

I have not followed these methods at all. On the contrary, I instinctively felt they would discourage me. Instead, at my entrance into religious life, I took a resolution to give myself up to God as the best satisfaction I could make for my sins and, for the love of Him, to renounce all besides.

For the first years, I commonly employed myself during the time set apart for devotion with thoughts of death, judgment, hell, heaven, and my sins. Thus, I continued some years applying my mind carefully the rest of the day, and even in the midst of my work, to the presence of God, whom I considered always as with me, often as in my heart.

At length I began to do the same thing during my set time of prayer, which gave me joy and consolation. This practice produced in me so high an esteem for God that faith alone was enough to assure me.

Such was my beginning. Yet I must tell you that for the first ten years I suffered a great deal. During this time, I fell often, and rose again presently. It seemed to me that all creatures, reason, and God Himself were against me and faith alone for me.

The apprehension that I was not devoted to God as I wished to be, my past sins always present to my mind, and the great unmerited favors which God did me, were the source of my sufferings and feelings of unworthiness. I was sometimes troubled with thoughts that to believe I had received such favors was an effect of my imagination, which pretended to be so soon where others arrived with great difficulty. At other times I believed that it was a willful delusion and that there really was no hope for me.

Finally, I considered the prospect of spending the rest of my days in these troubles. I discovered this did not diminish the trust I had in God at all. In fact, it only served to increase my faith. It then seemed that, all at once, I found myself changed. My soul, which, until that time was in trouble, felt a profound inward peace, as if she were in her center and place of rest.

Ever since that time I walk before God simply, in faith, with humility, and with love. I apply myself diligently to do nothing and think nothing which may displease Him. I hope that when I have done what I can, He will do with me what He pleases.

As for what passes in me at present, I cannot express it. I have no pain or difficulty about my state because I have no will but that of God. I endeavor to accomplish His will in all things. And I am so resigned that I would not take up a straw from the ground against His order or from any motive but that of pure love for Him.

I have ceased all forms of devotion and set prayers except those to which my state requires. I make it my priority to persevere in His holy presence, wherein I maintain a simple attention and a fond regard for God, which I may call an actual presence of God. Or, to put it another way, it is an habitual, silent, and private conversation of the soul with God. This gives me much joy and contentment. In short, I am sure, beyond all doubt, that my soul has been with God above these past thirty years. I pass over many things that I may not be tedious to you.

Yet, I think it is appropriate to tell you how I perceive myself before God, whom I behold as my King. I consider myself as the most wretched of men. I am full of faults, flaws, and weaknesses, and have committed all sorts of crimes against his King. Touched with a sensible regret I confess all my wickedness to Him. I ask His forgiveness. I abandon myself in His hands that He may do what He pleases with me.

My King is full of mercy and goodness. Far from chastising me, He embraces me with love. He makes me eat at His table. He serves me with His own hands and gives me the key to His treasures. He converses and delights Himself with me incessantly, in a thousand and a thousand ways. And He treats me in all respects as His favorite. In this way I consider myself continually in His holy presence.

My most usual method is this simple attention, an affectionate regard for God to whom I find myself often attached with greater sweetness and delight than that of an infant at the mother's breast. To choose an expression, I would call this state the bosom of God, for the inexpressible sweetness which I taste and experience there. If, at any time, my thoughts wander from it from necessity or infirmity, I am presently recalled by inward emotions so charming and delicious that I cannot find words to describe them. Please reflect on my great wretchedness, of which you are fully informed, rather than on the great favors God does one as unworthy and ungrateful as I am.

As for my set hours of prayer, they are simply a continuation of the same exercise. Sometimes I consider myself as a stone before a carver, whereof He is to make a statue. Presenting myself thus before God, I desire Him to make His perfect image in my soul and render me entirely like Himself. At other times, when I apply myself to prayer, I feel all my spirit lifted up without any care or effort on my part. This often continues as if it was suspended yet firmly fixed in God like a center or place of rest.

I know that some charge this state with inactivity, delusion, and self-love. I confess that it is a holy inactivity. And it would be a happy self-love if the soul, in that state, were capable of it. But while the soul is in this repose, she cannot be disturbed by the kinds of things to which she was formerly accustomed. The things that the soul used to depend on would now hinder rather than assist her.

Yet, I cannot see how this could be called imagination or delusion because the soul which enjoys God in this way wants nothing but Him. If this is delusion, then only God can remedy it. Let Him do what He pleases with me. I desire only Him and to be wholly devoted to Him.

Please send me your opinion as I greatly value and have a singular esteem for your reverence and am yours.

Third Letter

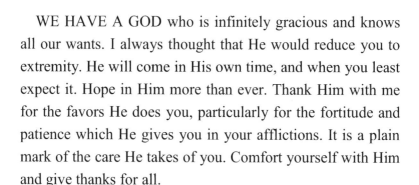

WE HAVE A GOD who is infinitely gracious and knows all our wants. I always thought that He would reduce you to extremity. He will come in His own time, and when you least expect it. Hope in Him more than ever. Thank Him with me for the favors He does you, particularly for the fortitude and patience which He gives you in your afflictions. It is a plain mark of the care He takes of you. Comfort yourself with Him and give thanks for all.

I admire also the fortitude and bravery of M——. God has given him a good disposition and a good will; but he is still a little worldly and somewhat immature. I hope the affliction God has sent him will help him do some reflection and inner searching and that it may prove to be a wholesome remedy to him. It is a chance for him to put all his trust in God who accompanies him everywhere. Let him think of Him as much as he can, especially in time of great danger.

A little lifting up of the heart and a remembrance of God suffices. One act of inward worship, though upon a march with sword in hand, are prayers which, however short, are nevertheless very acceptable to God. And, far from lessening a soldier's courage in occasions of danger, they actually serve to fortify it. Let him think of God as often as possible. Let him accustom himself, by degrees, to this small but holy exercise. No one sees it, and nothing is easier than to repeat these little internal adorations all through the day.

Please recommend to him that he think of God the most he can in this way. It is very fit and most necessary for a soldier, who is daily faced with danger to his life, and often to his very salvation.

I hope that God will assist him and all the family, to whom I present my service, being theirs and yours.

Fourth Letter

I AM TAKING THIS OPPORTUNITY to tell you about the sentiments of one of our society concerning the admirable effects and continual assistance he receives from the presence of God. May we both profit by them.

For the past forty years his continual care has been to be always with God; and to do nothing, say nothing, and think nothing which may displease Him. He does this without any view or motive except pure love of Him and because God deserves infinitely more.

He is now so accustomed to that Divine presence that he receives from it continual comfort and peace. For about thirty years his soul has been filled with joy and delight so continual, and sometimes so great, that he is forced to find ways to hide their appearing outwardly to others who may not understand.

If sometimes he becomes a little distracted from that Divine presence, God gently recalls Himself by a stirring in his soul. This often happens when he is most engaged in his outward chores and tasks. He answers with exact fidelity to these inward drawings, either by an elevation of his heart towards God, or by a meek and fond regard to Him, or by such words as love forms upon these occasions. For instance, he may say, "My God, here I am all devoted to You," or "Lord, make me according to Your heart."

It seems to him (in fact, he feels it) that this God of love, satisfied with such few words, reposes again and rests in the depth and center of his soul. The experience of these things gives him such certainty that God is always in the innermost part of his soul that he is beyond doubting it under any circumstances.

Judge by this what content and satisfaction he enjoys. While he continually finds within himself so great a treasure, he no longer has any need to search for it. He no longer has any anxiety about finding it because he now has his beautiful treasure open before him and may take what he pleases of it.

He often points out our blindness and exclaims that those who content themselves with so little are to be pitied. God, says he, has infinite treasure to bestow, and we take so little through routine devotion which lasts but a moment. Blind as we are, we hinder God, and stop the current of His graces. But when He finds a soul penetrated with a lively faith, He pours into it His graces and favors plentifully. There they flow like a torrent, which, after being forcibly stopped against its ordinary course, when it has found a passage, spreads itself with impetuosity and abundance.

Yet we often stop this torrent by the little value we set upon it. Let us stop it no more. Let us enter into ourselves and break down the bank which hinders it. Let us make way for grace. Let us redeem the lost time, for perhaps we have but little left. Death follows us close so let us be well prepared for it. We die but once and a mistake there is irretrievable.

I say again, let us enter into ourselves. The time presses. There is no room for delay. Our souls are at stake. It seems to me that you are prepared and have taken effectual measures so you will not be taken by surprise. I commend you for it. It is the one thing necessary. But those who have the gale of the Holy Spirit go forward even in sleep. If the vessel of our soul is still tossed with winds and storms, let us awake the Lord who reposes in it. He will quickly calm the sea.

I have taken the liberty to impart to you these good sentiments that you may compare them with your own. May they serve to re-kindle them, if at any time they may be even a little cooled. Let us recall our first favors and remember our early joys and comforts. And, let us benefit from the example and sentiments of this brother who is little known by the world, but known and extremely caressed by God.

I will pray for you. Please pray also for me, as I am yours in our Lord.

Fifth Letter

TODAY I RECEIVED TWO BOOKS and a letter from Sister M—, who is preparing to make her profession. She desires the prayers of your holy society, and yours in particular. I think she greatly values your support. Please do not disappoint her. Pray to God that she may take her vows in view of His love alone, and with a firm resolution to be wholly devoted to Him. I will send you one of those books about the presence of God; a subject which, in my opinion, contains the whole spiritual life. It seems to me that whoever duly practices it will soon become devout.

I know that for the right practice of it, the heart must be empty of all other things; because God will possess the heart alone. As He cannot possess it alone, without emptying it of all besides, so neither can He act there and do in it what He pleases unless it be left vacant to Him. There is not in the world a kind of life more sweet and delightful than that of a continual conversation with God. Only those can comprehend it who practice and experience it. Yet I do not advise you to do it from that motive. It is not pleasure which we ought to seek in this exercise. Let us do it from a principle of love, and because it is God's will for us.

Were I a preacher, I would above all other things preach the practice of the presence of God. Were I a director, I would advise all the world to do it, so necessary do I think it, and so easy too. Ah! knew we but the want we have of the grace and assistance of God, we would never lose sight of Him, no, not for a moment.

Believe me. Immediately make a holy and firm resolution never more to forget Him. Resolve to spend the rest of your days in His sacred presence, deprived of all consolations for the love of Him if He thinks fit. Set heartily about this work, and if you do it sincerely, be assured that you will soon find the effects of it.

I will assist you with my prayers, poor as they are. I recommend myself earnestly to you and those of your holy society.

Sixth Letter

I HAVE RECEIVED FROM M— the things which you gave her for me. I wonder that you have not given me your thoughts on the little book I sent to you and which you must have received. Set heartily about the practice of it in your old age. It is better late than never.

I cannot imagine how religious persons can live satisfied without the practice of the presence of God. For my part I keep myself retired with Him in the depth and center of my soul as much as I can. While I am with Him, I fear nothing; but the least turning from Him is insupportable. This practice does not tire the body. It is, however, proper to deprive it sometimes, nay often, of many little pleasures which are innocent and lawful. God will not permit a soul that desires to be devoted entirely to Him to take pleasures other than with Him. That is more than reasonable.

I do not say we must put any violent constraint upon ourselves. No, we must serve God in a holy freedom. We must work faithfully without trouble or disquiet, recalling our mind to God mildly and with tranquility as often as we find it wandering from Him. It is, however, necessary to put our whole trust in God. We must lay aside all other cares and even some forms of devotion, though very good in themselves, yet such as one often engages in routinely. Those devotions are only means to attain to the end. Once we have established a habit of the practice of the presence of God, we are then with Him who is our end. We have no need to return to the means. We may simply continue with Him in our commerce of love, persevering in His holy presence with an act of praise, of adoration, or of desire or with an act of resignation, or thanksgiving, and in all the ways our spirits can invent.

Be not discouraged by the repugnance which you may find in it from nature. You must sacrifice yourself. At first, one often thinks it a waste of time. But you must go on and resolve to persevere in it until death, notwithstanding all the difficulties that may occur.

I recommend myself to the prayers of your holy society, and yours in particular. I am yours in our Lord.

Seventh Letter

I PITY YOU MUCH. It will be a great relief if you can leave the care of your affairs to M— and spend the remainder of your life only in worshipping God. He requires no great matters of us; a little remembrance of Him from time to time, a little adoration. Sometimes to pray for His grace. Sometimes to offer Him your sufferings. And sometimes to return Him thanks for the favors He has given you, and still gives you, in the midst of your troubles. Console yourself with Him the oftenest you can. Lift up your heart to Him at your meals and when you are in company. The least little remembrance will always be pleasing to Him.

You need not cry very loud. He is nearer to us than we are aware. And we do not always have to be in church to be with God. We may make an oratory of our heart so we can, from time to time, retire to converse with Him in meekness, humility, and love. Everyone is capable of such familiar conversation with God, some more, some less. He knows what we can do.

Let us begin then. Perhaps He expects but one generous resolution on our part. Have courage. We have but little time to live. You are nearly sixty-four, and I am almost eighty. Let us live and die with God. Sufferings will be sweet and pleasant while we are with Him. Without Him, the greatest pleasures will be a cruel punishment to us. May He be blessed by all.

Gradually become accustomed to worship Him in this way; to beg His grace, to offer Him your heart from time to time; in the midst of your business, even every moment if you can. Do not always scrupulously confine yourself to certain rules or particular forms of devotion. Instead, act in faith with love and humility.

You may assure M— of my poor prayers, and that I am their servant, and yours particularly.

Eighth Letter

YOU TELL ME NOTHING NEW. You are not the only one who is troubled with wandering thoughts. Our mind is extremely roving. But the will is mistress of all our faculties. She must recall our stray thoughts and carry them to God as their final end.

If the mind is not sufficiently controlled and disciplined at our first engaging in devotion, it contracts certain bad habits of wandering and dissipation. These are difficult to overcome. The mind can draw us, even against our will, to worldly things. I believe one remedy for this is to humbly confess our faults and beg God's mercy and help.

I do not advise you to use multiplicity of words in prayer. Many words and long discourses are often the occasions of wandering. Hold yourself in prayer before God, like a dumb or paralytic beggar at a rich man's gate. Let it be your business to keep your mind in the presence of the Lord. If your mind sometimes wanders and withdraws itself from Him, do not become upset. Trouble and disquiet serve rather to distract the mind than to re-collect it. The will must bring it back in tranquility. If you persevere in this manner, God will have pity on you.

One way to re-collect the mind easily in the time of prayer, and preserve it more in tranquility, is not to let it wander too far at other times. Keep your mind strictly in the presence of

God. Then being accustomed to think of Him often, you will find it easy to keep your mind calm in the time of prayer, or at least to recall it from its wanderings. I have told you already of the advantages we may draw from this practice of the presence of God. Let us set about it seriously and pray for one another.

Ninth Letter

THE ENCLOSED IS AN ANSWER to that which I received from M—. Please deliver it to her. She is full of good will, but she would go faster than grace! One does not become holy all at once. I recommend her to your guidance. We ought to help one another by our advice, and yet more by our good example. Please let me hear of her from time to time and whether she is very fervent and obedient.

Let us often consider that our only business in this life is to please God, that perhaps all besides is but folly and vanity. You and I have lived over forty years in the monastic life. Have we employed them in loving and serving God, who by His mercy has called us to this state and for that very end? I am sometimes filled with shame and confusion when I reflect, on the one hand, upon the great favors which God has done and continues to do for me; and, on the other, upon the ill-use I have made of them and my small advancement in the way of perfection.

Since, by His mercy, He gives us yet a little time, let us begin in earnest. Let us repair the lost time. Let us return with full assurance to that Father of mercies, who is always ready to receive us affectionately. Let us generously renounce, for the love of Him, all that is not Himself. He deserves infinitely more. Let us think of Him perpetually. Let us put all our trust in Him.

I have no doubt that we shall soon receive an abundance of His grace, with which we can do all things, and, without which we can do nothing but sin. We cannot escape the dangers which abound in life without the actual and continual help of God. Let us pray to Him for it constantly.

How can we pray to Him without being with Him? How can we be with Him but in thinking of Him often? And how can we often think of Him, but by a holy habit which we should form of it? You will tell me that I always say the same thing. It is true, for this is the best and easiest method I know. I use no other. I advise all the world to do it.

We must know before we can love. In order to know God, we must often think of Him. And when we come to love Him, we shall then also think of Him often, for our heart will be with our treasure.

Tenth Letter

I HAVE HAD A GOOD DEAL of difficulty bringing myself to write to M.—. I do it now purely because you desire me to do so. Please address it and send it to him. It is pleasing to see all the faith you have in God. May He increase it in you more and more. We cannot have too much trust in so good and faithful a Friend who will never fail us in this world nor in the next.

If M.— takes advantage of the loss he has had and puts all his confidence in God, He will soon give him another friend more powerful and more inclined to serve him. He disposes of hearts as He pleases. Perhaps M.— was too attached to him he has lost. We ought to love our friends, but without encroaching upon the love of God, which must always be first.

Please keep my recommendation in mind that you think of God often; by day, by night, in your business, and even in your diversions. He is always near you and with you. Leave Him not alone. You would think it rude to leave a friend alone who came to visit you. Why, then, must God be neglected? Do not forget Him but think on Him often. Adore Him continually. Live and die with Him. This is the glorious work of a Christian; in a word, this is our profession. If we do not know it, we must learn it.

I will endeavor to help you with my prayers and am yours in our Lord.

Eleventh Letter

I DO NOT PRAY that you may be delivered from your pains; but I pray earnestly that God gives you strength and patience to bear them as long as He pleases. Comfort yourself with Him who holds you fastened to the cross. He will loose you when He thinks fit. Happy are those who suffer with Him. Accustom yourself to suffer in that manner and seek from Him the strength to endure as much, and as long, as He judges necessary for you.

Worldly people do not comprehend these truths. It is not surprising though, since they suffer like what they are and not like Christians. They see sickness as a pain against nature and not as a favor from God. Seeing it only in that light, they find nothing in it but grief and distress. But those who consider sickness as coming from the hand of God, out of His mercy and as the means He uses for their salvation, commonly find sweetness and consolation in it.

I pray that you see that God is often nearer to us and present within us in sickness than in health. Do not rely completely on another physician because He reserves your cure to Himself. Put all your trust in God. You will soon find the effects in your recovery, which we often delay by putting greater faith in medicine than in God. Whatever remedies you use, they will succeed only so far as He permits. When pains come from God, only He can ultimately cure them. He often sends sickness to the body to cure diseases of the soul. Comfort yourself with the Sovereign Physician of both soul and body.

I expect you will say that I am very much at ease, and that I eat and drink at the table of the Lord. You have reason. But think how painful it would be to the greatest criminal in the world to eat at the king's table and be served by him, yet have no assurance of pardon? I believe he would feel an anxiety that nothing could calm except his trust in the goodness of his sovereign. So, I assure you, that whatever pleasures I taste at the table of my King, my sins, ever present before my eyes, as well as the uncertainty of my pardon, torment me. Though I accept that torment as something pleasing to God.

Be satisfied with the condition in which God places you. However happy you may think me, I envy you. Pain and suffering would be a paradise to me, if I could suffer with my God. The greatest pleasures would be hell if I relished them without Him. My only consolation would be to suffer something for His sake.

I must, in a little time, go to God. What comforts me in this life is that I now see Him by faith. I see Him in such a manner that I sometimes say, I believe no more, but I see. I feel what faith teaches us, and, in that assurance and that practice of faith, I live and die with Him.

Stay with God always for He is the only support and comfort for your affliction. I shall beseech Him to be with you. I present my service.

Twelfth Letter

IF WE WERE WELL ACCUSTOMED to the practice of the presence of God, bodily discomforts would be greatly alleviated. God often permits us to suffer a little to purify our souls and oblige us to stay close to Him.

Take courage. Offer Him your pain and pray to Him for strength to endure them. Above all, get in the habit of often thinking of God, and forget Him the least you can. Adore Him in your infirmities. Offer yourself to Him from time to time. And, in the height of your sufferings, humbly and affectionately beseech Him (as a child his father) to make you conformable to His holy will. I shall endeavor to assist you with my poor prayers.

God has many ways of drawing us to Himself. He sometimes seems to hide Himself from us. But faith alone ought to be our support. Faith is the foundation of our confidence. We must put all our faith in God. He will not fail us in time of need. I do not know how God will dispose of me but I am always happy. All the world suffers and I, who deserve the severest discipline, feel joys so continual and great that I can scarcely contain them.

I would willingly ask God for a part of your sufferings. I know my weakness is so great that if He left me one moment to myself, I would be the most wretched man alive. And yet, I do not know how He could leave me alone because faith gives me as strong a conviction as reason. He never forsakes us until we have first forsaken Him. Let us fear to leave Him. Let us always be with Him. Let us live and die in His presence. Do pray for me, as I pray for you.

Thirteenth Letter

I AM SORRY TO SEE YOU SUFFER so long. What gives me some ease and sweetens the feeling I have about your griefs, is that they are proof of God's love for you. See your pains in that view and you will bear them more easily. In your case, it is my opinion that, at this point, you should discontinue human remedies and resign yourself entirely to the providence of God. Perhaps He waits only for that resignation and perfect faith in Him to cure you. Since, in spite of all the care you have taken, treatment has proved unsuccessful and your malady still increases, wait no longer. Put yourself entirely in His hands and expect all from Him.

I told you in my last letter that He sometimes permits bodily discomforts to cure the distempers of the soul. Have courage. Make a virtue of necessity. Do not ask God for deliverance from your pain. Instead, out of love for Him, ask for the strength to resolutely bear all that He pleases, and as long as He pleases. Such prayers are hard at first, but they are very pleasing to God, and become sweet to those that love Him.

Love sweetens pains. And when one loves God, one suffers for His sake with joy and courage. Do so, I beseech you. Comfort yourself with Him. He is the only physician for all our illnesses. He is the Father of the afflicted and always ready to help us. He loves us infinitely more than we can imagine. Love Him in return and seek no consolation elsewhere. I hope you will soon receive His comfort. Adieu.

I will help you with my prayers, poor as they are, and shall always be yours in our Lord.

Fourteenth Letter

I GIVE THANKS to our Lord for having relieved you a little as you desired. I have often been near death and I was never so much satisfied as then. At those times I did not pray for any relief, but I prayed for strength to suffer with courage, humility, and love. How sweet it is to suffer with God! However great your sufferings may be, receive them with love. It is paradise to suffer and be with Him. If, in this life, we might enjoy the peace of paradise, we must accustom ourselves to a familiar, humble, and affectionate conversation with God.

We must hinder our spirits wandering from Him on all occasions. We must make our heart a spiritual temple so we can constantly adore Him. We must continually watch over ourselves so we do not do anything that may displease Him. When our minds and hearts are filled with God, suffering becomes full of unction and consolation.

I well know that to arrive at this state, the beginning is very difficult because we must act purely on faith. But, though it is difficult, we know also that we can do all things with the grace of God. He never refuses those who ask earnestly. Knock. Persevere in knocking. And I answer for it, that, in His due time, He will open His graces to you. He will grant, all at once, what He has deferred during many years. Adieu.

Pray to Him for me, as I pray to Him for you. I hope to see Him soon.

Fifteenth Letter

GOD KNOWS BEST WHAT WE NEED. All that He does is for our good. If we knew how much He loves us, we would always be ready to receive both the bitter and the sweet from His Hand. It would make no difference. All that came from Him would be pleasing. The worst afflictions only appear intolerable if we see them in the wrong light. When we see them as coming from the hand of God and know that it is our loving Father who humbles and distresses us, our sufferings lose their bitterness and can even become a source of consolation.

Let all our efforts be to know God. The more one knows Him, the greater one desires to know Him. Knowledge is commonly the measure of love. The deeper and more extensive our knowledge, the greater is our love. If our love of God were great, we would love Him equally in pain and pleasure.

We only deceive ourselves by seeking or loving God for any favors which He has or may grant us. Such favors, no matter how great, can never bring us as near to God as can one simple act of faith. Let us seek Him often by faith. He is within us. Seek Him not elsewhere.

Are we not rude and deserve blame if we leave Him alone to busy ourselves with trifles which do not please Him and perhaps even offend Him? These trifles may one day cost us dearly. Let us begin earnestly to be devoted to Him. Let us cast everything else out of our hearts. He wants to possess the heart alone. Beg this favor of Him. If we do all we can, we will soon see that change wrought in us which we so greatly desire.

I cannot thank Him enough for the relief He has given you. I hope to see Him within a few days. Let us pray for one another.

Brother Lawrence died peacefully within days of this last letter.

Leave a Review

Thank you again for reading this book! I hope and pray that in some way it encouraged you to grow closer to Christ.

If you enjoyed this book, I would appreciate your leaving an honest review for the book and study on Amazon! Your review will help others know if this study is right for them and their small group.

It's easy and will only take a minute. Just search for "The Practice of the Presence of God, Alan Vermilye" on Amazon. Click on the product in the search results, and then click on reviews.

I would also love to hear from you! Drop me a note by visiting me at www.BrownChairBooks.com and clicking on "Contact."

Thank you and God bless!

Alan

Other Studies from Brown Chair Books

On the following pages, you'll descriptions and reviews from
some of our other Bible studies.

www.BrownChairBooks.com

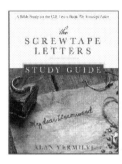

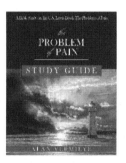

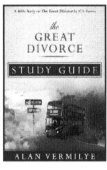

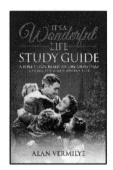

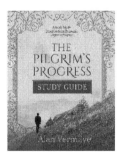

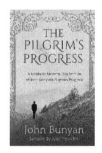

THE PILGRIM'S PROGRESS BOOK AND STUDY GUIDE
By Alan Vermilye

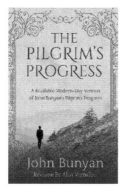

Reading *The Pilgrim's Progress* by John Bunyan can be a bit challenging even for the best of readers. Not so with this new, easy-to-read version that translates the original archaic language into simple conversational English allowing readers of all ages to easily navigate the most popular Christian allegory of all time.

The story chronicles the epic adventure of a man named Christian who leaves his home in the City of Destruction and begins a life-long quest to the Celestial City. Set against the backdrop of a hazardous journey, this powerful drama unfolds as Christian's adventures lead him into fascinating lands and encounters with interesting people who either help or hinder his progress along a narrow way.

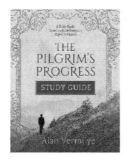

This comprehensive Bible study workbook will guide you through Bunyan's masterful use of metaphors helping you better understand key concepts, supporting Bible passages, and the relevance to our world today.

MERE CHRISTIANITY STUDY GUIDE
A Bible Study on the C.S. Lewis Book *Mere Christianity*
By Steven Urban

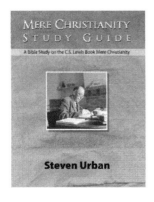

Mere Christianity Study Guide takes participants through a study of C.S. Lewis's classic *Mere Christianity*. Yet despite its recognition as a "classic," there is surprisingly little available today in terms of a serious study course.

This 12-week Bible study digs deep into each chapter and, in turn, into Lewis's thoughts. Perfect for small group sessions, this interactive workbook includes daily, individual study as well as a complete appendix and commentary to supplement and further clarify certain topics. Multiple week format options are also included.

What others are saying:

This study guide is more than just a guide to C.S Lewis' Mere Christianity; *it is a guide to Christianity itself.* – Crystal

Wow! What a lot of insight and food for thought! Perfect supplement to Mere Christianity. *I think Mr. Lewis himself would approve.* – Laurie

Our group is in the middle of studying Mere Christianity, *and I have found this guide to be invaluable.*
– Angela

THE SCREWTAPE LETTERS STUDY GUIDE
A Bible Study on the C.S. Lewis Book
The Screwtape Letters
By Alan Vermilye

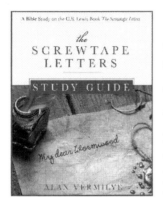

The Screwtape Letters Study Guide takes participants through a study of C.S. Lewis's classic, *The Screwtape Letters.*

This Bible study digs deep into each letter from Screwtape, an undersecretary in the lowerarchy of Hell, to his incompetent nephew Wormwood, a junior devil. Perfect for small group sessions, this interactive workbook includes daily, individual study with a complete answer guide available online.

Designed as a 12-week study, multiple-week format options are also included.

What others are saying:

This book and study creates a positive reinforcement on fighting that spiritual battle in life. Great read, great study guide! – Lester

This study guide was a wonderful way for our group to work through The Screwtape Letters! – Becky

Use this study guide for a fresh "seeing" of The Screwtape Letters! – William

THE GREAT DIVORCE STUDY GUIDE
A Bible Study on the C.S. Lewis Book *The Great Divorce*
By Alan Vermilye

The Great Divorce Study Guide is an eight-week Bible study on the C.S. Lewis classic, *The Great Divorce*. Perfect for small groups or individual study, each weekly study session applies a biblical framework to the concepts found in each chapter of the book. Although intriguing and entertaining, much of Lewis's writings can be difficult to grasp.

The Great Divorce Study Guide will guide you through each one of Lewis's masterful metaphors to a better understanding of the key concepts of the book, the supporting Bible passages, and the relevance to our world today. Each study question is ideal for group discussion, and answers to each question are available online.

What others are saying:

To my knowledge, there have not been many study guides for either of these, so to see this new one on The Great Divorce *(both electronic and print) is a welcome sight!* – Richard

I recommend The Great Divorce Study Guide *to anyone or any group wishing to delve more deeply into the question, why would anyone choose hell over heaven!* – Ruth

THE PROBLEM OF PAIN STUDY GUIDE

A Bible Study on the C.S. Lewis Book *The Problem of Pain*
By Alan Vermilye

 In his book, *The Problem of Pain*, C.S. Lewis's philosophical approach to why we experience pain can be confusing at times. *The Problem of Pain Study Guide* breaks down each chapter into easy-to-understand questions and commentary to help you find meaning and hope amid the pain.

The Problem of Pain Study Guide expands upon Lewis's elegant and thoughtful work, where he seeks to understand how a loving, good, and powerful God can possibly coexist with the pain and suffering that is so pervasive in the world and in our lives. As Christ-followers we might expect the world to be just, fair, and less painful, but it is not. This is the problem of pain.

What others are saying:

Many thanks for lending me a helping hand with one of the greatest thinkers of all time! – Adrienne

The questions posed range from very straightforward (to help the reader grasp main concepts) to more probing (to facilitate personal application), while perhaps the greatest benefit they supply is their tie-in of coordinating scriptures that may not always be apparent to the reader. – Sphinn

A CHRISTMAS CAROL STUDY GUIDE
Book and Bible Study Based on *A Christmas Carol*
By Alan Vermilye

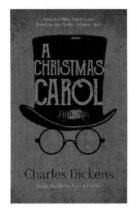

A Christmas Carol Book and Bible Study Guide includes the entire book of this Dickens classic as well as Bible study discussion questions for each chapter, Scripture references, and related commentary.

Detailed character sketches and an easy-to-read book summary provide deep insights into each character while examining the book's themes of greed, isolation, guilt, blame, compassion, generosity, transformation, forgiveness, and, finally, redemption. To help with those more difficult discussion questions, a complete answer guide is available for free online.

What others are saying:

The study is perfect for this time of the year, turning our focus to the reason for the season—Jesus—and the gift of redemption we have through him. – Connie

I used this for an adult Sunday School class. We all loved it! – John

This study is wonderful! – Lori

I found this a refreshing look at the Bible through the eyes of Ebenezer Scrooge's life. – Lynelle

IT'S A WONDERFUL STUDY GUIDE
A Bible Study Based on the Christmas Classic *It's a Wonderful Life*
By Alan Vermilye

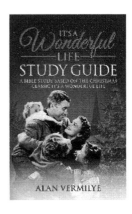

It's a Wonderful Life is one of the most popular and heart-warming films ever made. It's near-universal appeal and association with Christmas has provided a rich story of redemption that has inspired generations for decades.

It's a Wonderful Life Study Guide examines this beloved holiday classic and reminds us how easily we can become distracted from what is truly meaningful in life. This five-week Bible study experience comes complete with discussion questions for each session, Scripture references, detailed character sketches, movie summary, and related commentary. In addition, a complete answer guide and video segments for each session are available for free online.

What others are saying:

Thank you, Alan, for the unforgettable experience. Your book has prompted me to see and learn much more than merely enjoying the film, It's a Wonderful Life. – Er Jwee

The questions got us all thinking, and the answers provided were insightful and encouraging. I would definitely encourage Home Groups to study this! – Jill

It's a Wonderful Life Study Guide *by Alan Vermilye is intelligent, innovative, interesting, involving, insightful, and inspirational.* – Paul